ARF!

P9-AZV-948

Hey, baby.

You know, there are lots of you babies out there, each with your own face, your own hair, and your own little butt. That's right, you got your own squishy tushy with its own special shape. See, you babies and your butts come in beautiful shapes and sizes. And we believe each one should squiggle, wiggle, and jiggle around freely. In fact, we wrote the book on that. Literally. So here's to the gazillion shapes of babies and butts out there. Or at least twenty-six of them, this being an alphabet book and all.

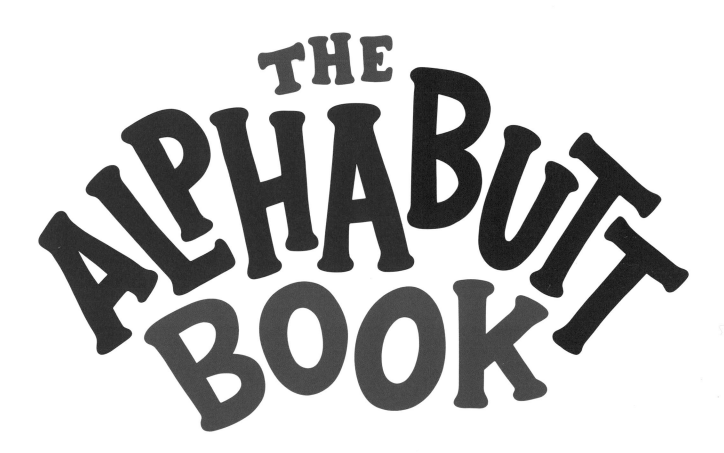

The Alphabut Book

An **ABCs** of Baby Butts & Bodies

 **HUGGIES**

National Diaper Bank Network

 sourcebooks eXplore

A
is for

Avocado Butt

And all the awesome acrobatic-y things it can achieve

Teresa Bellón • @teresa_bellon

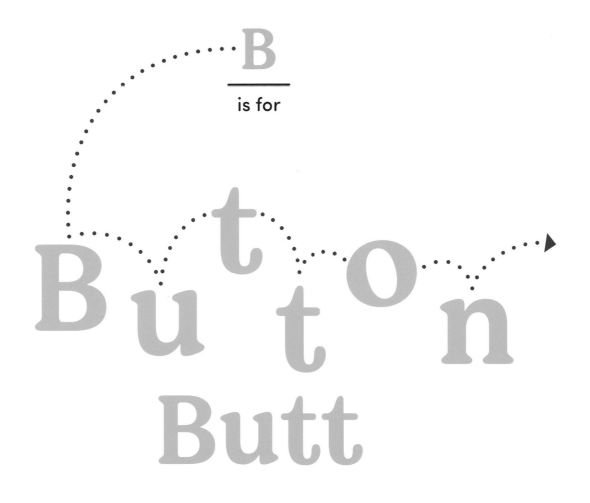

B is for

Button
Butt

Bouncing blissfully before
a big ol' bubble bath

Gemma Correll • @gemmacorrell

C

is for

Chasing chatty chihuahuas
in Chattanooga

JooHee Yoon • jooheeyoon.com

D is for

Daddy Long Legs
Butt

Doing a disco dance with
Daddy to dynomite ditties

Zachariah OHora • @fuzzytown

E

is for

Eggy Butt

Exhausting everyone with its endless energy

Christoph Niemann • @abstractsunday

F

is for

Flamingo Butt

Frolicking freely with its floppy feet

Mathias Ball • @snurkyduck

G

is for

Gigantasaurus Butt

Goofily galloping at the
ginormous gymnasium

Jasmine Floyd • @jasminefloyd

H

is for

Herculean

Butt

Hopping around saying
"howdy" with its huge hands

Christiane Engel • @chengel_illustration

I

is for

Itty

Bitty

Butt

Imagining it is impressively
ice skating indoors

Sarah Andersen • @sarahandersencomics

J

is for

Jiggly Jelly Butt

Jingle-jangling while
joyously jumping

Tyler Feder • @tylerfeder

K

is for

Knee-High Butt

Known for its kooky karate kicks
and occasional K9 karaoke

Flavia Z. Drago • @flavia_zdrago

L
is for

Lopsided
Butt

Laughing while leaping into
large lumps of laundry

Erika Lynne Jones • @erikalynnejones

M
is for

Munchkin Butt

Moving merrily past Mommy while
munching meatless mostaccioli

Tisha Lee • @tishalee_art

N

is for

No Butt Butt

Noisily noodling in the nursery at naptime

Heegyum Kim • @hee_cookingdiary

O
___
is for

Old Man Butt

Outrunning other one-year-olds
as onlookers say "oooooh"

Elise Gravel • @elise_gravel

P

is for

Pillowy
Butt

Playfully pouncing upon its
pooped parents

Jeremyville • @jeremyville

Q

is for

QUADRI
LATERAL
Butt

On a quest to become a
highly-qualified quarterback queen

Jana Glatt • @janaglatt

R

is for

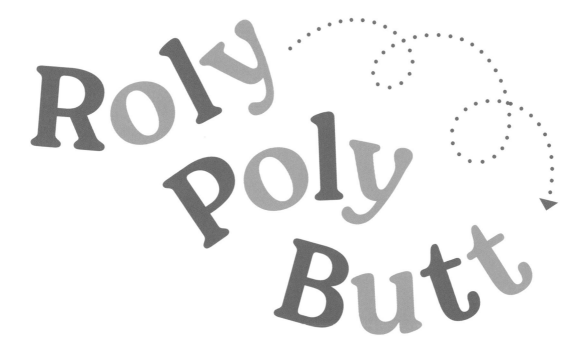

Roly Poly Butt

Rambunctiously rocking that
rump round 'n' round

Keith Negley • @keith_negley

is for

String
Beany
Butt

Strutting like a silly-pants in
super, stripy socks

Grand Chamaco • @grand_chamaco

T
is for

Tater Tot Butt

Twisting its tushy while
tooting to-and-fro

Jason Grube • @grubedoo

U

is for

Unicorn
Butt

Which, left unattended, may
unfortunately upend all upholstery

Juan Molinet • @molinetjuan

V

is for

Viking Butt

Vertically vaulting over a
very loud-volume vacuum

Chaaya Prabhat • @chaaya23

W

is for

W
E E
N S Y

Teensy Butt

Weirdly wiggly-waggling with a wedge of watermelon

Craig & Karl • @craigandkarl

X

is for

X-tra
SQUISHY
Butt

X-citedly x-pressing itself
on the xylophone

Vanessa Brantley-Newton • @vanessabrantleynewton

Y

is for

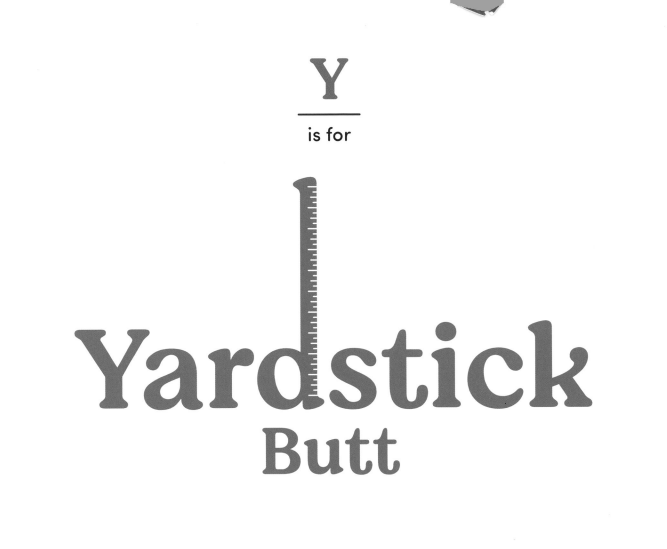

Yardstick
Butt

Yoga-ing like a yo-yo while
yammering "yippee yay yahoo!"

Alice Piaggio • @alicepiaggio_illustratrice

Z
is for

Butt

Zigging and zagging like a
zany, zonked-out zombie

Brosmind • @brosmind

Alphabutt Artists

from A to Zz^zz^zz

D

Zachariah OHora
@fuzzytown

E

Christoph
Niemann
@abstractsunday

F

Mathias Ball
@sulkypup

J

Tyler Feder
@tylerfeder

K

Flavia Z. Drago
@flavia_zdrago

L

Erika Lynne Jones
@erikalynnejones

P

Jeremyville
@jeremyville

Q

Jana Glatt
@janaglatt

R

Keith Negley
@keith_negley

V

Chaaya Prabhat
@chaaya23

W

Craig & Karl
@craigandkarl

X

Vanessa
Brantley-Newton
@vanessa
brantleynewton

A
Teresa Bellón
@teresa_bellon

B
Gemma Correll
@gemmacorrell

C
JooHee Yoon
jooheeyoon.com

G
Jasmine Floyd
@jasminefloyd

H
Christiane Engel
@chengel_
illustration

I
Sarah Andersen
@sarahanders
encomics

M
Tisha Lee
@tishalee_art

N
Heegyum Kim
@hee_
cookingdiary

O
Elise Gravel
@elise_gravel

S
Grand Chamaco
@grand_
chamaco

T
Jason Grube
@grubedoo

U
Juan Molinet
@molinetjuan

Y
Alice Piaggio
@alicepiaggio_
illustratrice

Z
Brosmind
@brosmind

Cover
Jason Grube
@grubedoo

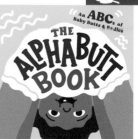

Leave No Butts Behind

Not only did we want to make a book about baby butts, but we also wanted to help cover every butt in need. So a portion of the proceeds of *The Alphabutt Book* go to the National Diaper Bank Network, a nonprofit working to end diaper need in the U.S. by providing diapers and other basic necessities to struggling families. Because every baby butt in the world deserves to feel safe and cozy.

To learn more, visit nationaldiaperbanknetwork.org

 X **National Diaper Bank Network**

Text and illustrations copyright © 2023 by Kimberly-Clark Worldwide, Inc.
Concepted & written by QualityMeatsCreative.com
Editorial Consultation by Alli Brydon
Design by Headquarters.studio
Illustrations by Teresa Bellón, Gemma Correll, JooHee Yoon, Zachariah OHora,
Christoph Niemann, Mathias Ball, Jasmine Floyd, Christiane Engel, Sarah Andersen,
Tyler Feder, Flavia Z. Drago, Erika Lynne Jones, Tisha Lee, Heegyum Kim, Elise Gravel,
Jeremyville, Jana Glatt, Keith Negley, Grand Chamaco, Jason Grube, Juan Molinet,
Chaaya Prabhat, Craig & Karl, Vanessa Brantley Newton, Alice Piaggio, Brosmind
Cover and internal design © 2023 by Sourcebooks

Sourcebooks and the colophon are registered trademarks of Sourcebooks.

All rights reserved.

The characters and events portrayed in this book are fictitious or
are used fictitiously. Any similarity to real persons, living or dead,
is purely coincidental and not intended by the author.

All brand names and product names used in this book are trademarks,
registered trademarks, or trade names of their respective holders. Sourcebooks
is not associated with any product or vendor in this book.

Published by Sourcebooks eXplore, an imprint of Sourcebooks Kids
P.O. Box 4410, Naperville, Illinois 60567-4410
(630) 961-3900
sourcebookskids.com

Cataloging-in-Publication Data is on file with the Library of Congress.

Source of Production: Phoenix Color, Hagerstown, Maryland, USA
Date of Production: July 2023
Run Number: 5033265

Printed and bound in the United States of America.
PHC 10 9 8 7 6 5 4 3 2 1